Contents

Doable 1 – Opening an Account

Doable 2 – Settings

Doable 3 – Background Design

Doable 4 – Start Connecting

Doable 5 – Retweeting and Favorites

Doable 6 – What to Post

Doable 7 – Posting

Doable 8 – @mentions, @replies and DMs

Doable 9 – Scheduling Tools

Doable 10 – Hashtags (#)

Doable 11 – Lists

Doable 12 – Building Relationships Using Lists

Doable 13 – Link Shorteners

Doable 14 – Twitter Search

Doable 15 – Finding People to Follow

Doable 16 – Starting Conversations

Doable 17 – Saying Thank You

Doable 18 – Be Retweetable

Doable 19 – #FollowFriday

Doable 20 – Best Time to Post

Doable 21 – Posting Images

Doable 22 – Trends

Doable 23 – Website Widgets

Doable 24 – Adding an Additional Link in Your Bio

Doable 25 – Linking to Individual Tweets

Doable 26 – Managing Who You Follow

Doable 27 – Promoting Your Account

Doable 28 – Mobile Applications

Doable 29 – Twitter Time Management

Doable 30 – Congratulations!

Doable 1 – Opening an Account

It is a very simple process to open an account on Twitter. Go to www.Twitter.com and you will find a page that looks something like the one below. Add your name, email and password and click sign up.

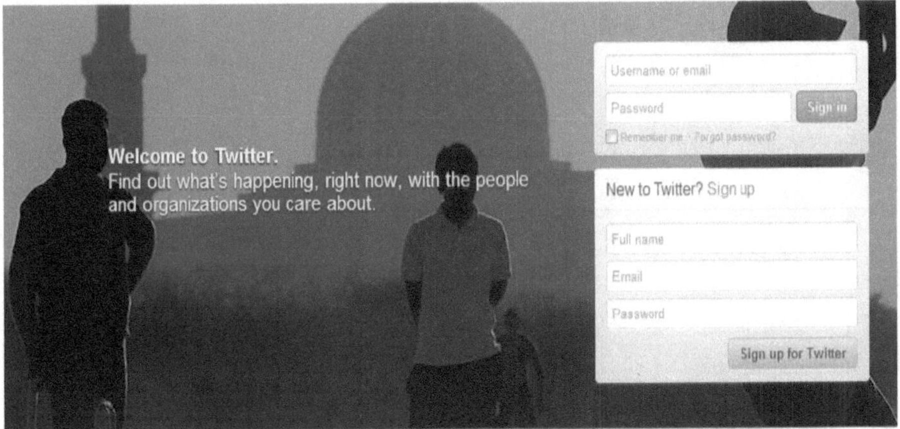

Join Twitter today.

Full name

Enter your first and last name.

Email address

Create a password

Choose your username

☑ Keep me signed-in on this computer.

By clicking the button, you agree to the terms below:

These Terms of Service ("Terms") govern your access to and use of the services, including our various websites, SMS, APIs, email notifications,

Printable versions:
Terms of Service · Privacy Policy

Create my account

Note: Others will be able to find you by name, username or email. Your email will not be shown publicly. You can change your privacy settings at any time.

On this next page you will supply other information about yourself including a username.

Type in the username you want, to see if it is available. As more people sign up to Twitter the harder it is to get your own name. I wanted staceymyers but it wasn't available, so I had to go for staceylmyers instead. Ideally you don't want to use an underscore (_) or number, but sometimes it is unavoidable.

If you are a big business then use your business name, if not, I recommend using your own name. This makes it easy for people to find you.

Your username then becomes your Twitter URL -

http://www.twitter.com/username. This is what you use when promoting your account. When people visit that link it takes them straight to your profile page on Twitter.

You can change your username at any time, but you will have a new address and will need to notify people that you have a new username, so it is much easier to get it right in the first place.

Doable 2 – Settings

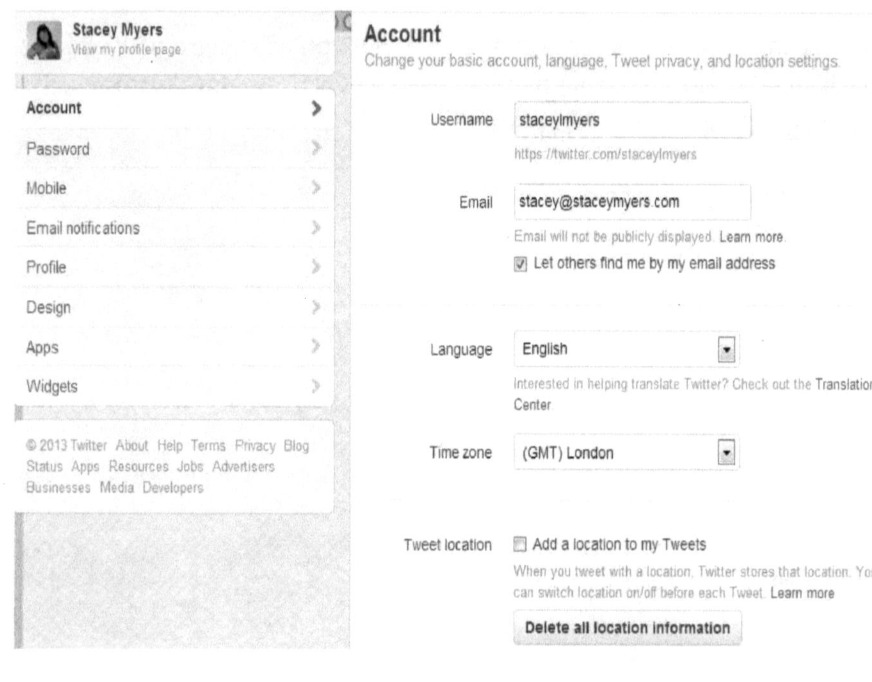

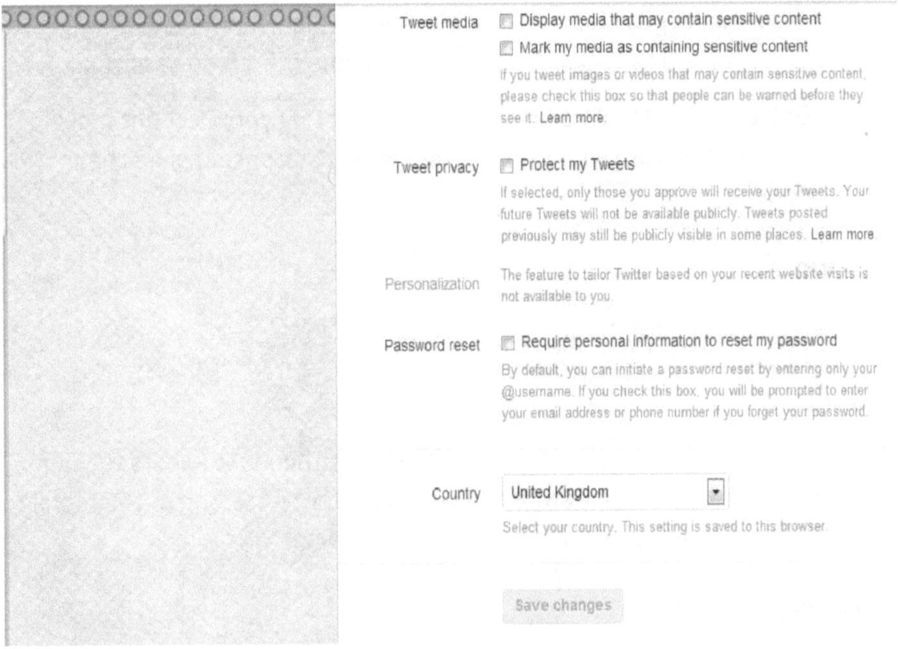

Tweet media Display media that may contain sensitive content

Mark my media as containing sensitive content

If you tweet images or videos that may contain sensitive content, please check this box so that people can be warned before they see it. Learn more.

Tweet privacy Protect my Tweets

If selected, only those you approve will receive your Tweets. Your future Tweets will not be available publicly. Tweets posted previously may still be publicly visible in some places. Learn more.

Personalization The feature to tailor Twitter based on your recent website visits is not available to you.

Password reset Require personal information to reset my password

By default, you can initiate a password reset by entering only your @username. If you check this box, you will be prompted to enter your email address or phone number if you forget your password.

Country United Kingdom

Select your country. This setting is saved to this browser.

Save changes

Let's look at each tab in turn:

Account Tab:

- **Username -** This is the username you used to open your account. If you ever want to change your username this is where to do it.

- **Rest of Fields -** Most of the fields have explanations inside the dashboard. There are, however, a few things to note:

  - It is desirable to identify a 'location' on your bio so people searching for a service in your area can easily find you. However, I discourage you from including a location from within each tweet, so leave this box unchecked.

  - It will depend how you plan to use Twitter if you want your tweets to be private or public. If you're using it for business and pleasure keep the tweets unlocked.
  If you lock your tweets it means those who wish to follow you must get your approval first. This is definitely not ideal if you are looking to build a community. It could be perceived as

being guarded and is a lot of upkeep on your end. Having locked tweets will keep some people from following you.

- **Delete Account** - Of course if you are deleting your account make sure that you are sure! There is no going back once this has been done.

Password:

Change your password here.

Mobile:

You can add your phone number in here and can then text tweets to your account. I do not use this feature as I would prefer to use one of the mobile applications that are available (more on that later).

Email Notifications:

You can set up various alerts to be emailed to you. For example, when someone new follows you, if you receive a DM, or Twitter updates. I have all of these turned off. I am on Twitter every day so I can see what is going on. If you are only going to Twitter occasionally then you might want to set up some notifications. You can change the settings at any time.

Profile:

Your profile picture –

NO EGGHEADS! An egghead is the generic image Twitter gives you when you open your account. Twitter is about building relationships and no one wants to interact with an egghead. Upload a picture of yourself – not your pet or your favourite flower or cartoon character. Having a photo of yourself makes your profile seem more personable and memorable to other users. People naturally like to put a face to a name. If you are a big company it is generally fine to put up a company logo but if you are a small business it is better to have your own photo there. Your profile image shows up beside your tweets.

Header Image:

The header is the larger image behind the profile image on your home page. Some people really brand this area but I personally do not think it is a good idea, especially if you already have a branded background (more about the background in the next Doable). I have used an image from my trip to South Africa. If you do not upload your own image Twitter will assign you a dark grey one.

Name -

It is best to use your real name here. Especially if you are not using your name as your @username.

Location -

People like to know whereabouts you are so make sure you fill this in. This is also useful when looking for people in a certain area.

Website -

Enter a website address here. This can be any website you choose – it could be your blog, your Facebook page or a link to a free gift you are offering. Do make sure you fill this in though, because it can provide you with an excellent source of traffic.

Bio -

When writing your Twitter bio, it's important to ensure you are sending the same message on Twitter as you do on other platforms, such as Facebook and LinkedIn.

In fewer than 160 characters write something about yourself. Keywords are important based on your niche, product or service provided. The words you use should be based on the type of Twitter followers you want to attract. Twitter users are able to search other users based on the words in their bio.

Your Twitter bio can include:

- A word that describes how you see yourself - Entrepreneur
- Your personal interests and likes - fisherman at heart, coffee lover
- What you do as a business or for clients - jewelry maker, social media
- Your niche - copywriting, social media manager, author, writer

Facebook -

It is not a good idea to link your Twitter account to your Facebook page or profile. Tweets are not really appropriate on there for a few reasons. @mentions look out of place when you see them in a Facebook post and most people post more times in a day on Twitter than on Facebook, so it can get to be a bit much. You can, however, connect Facebook to Twitter so when you post on Facebook it also posts on Twitter. You can do that at www.facebook.com/twitter.

Apps:

These are all the places you have allowed a 3rd party application to connect with your Twitter account. Whenever you use Twitter to log in to a website or when you share from someone's website it will ask for permission to access your Twitter account – this is how they turn up in your Twitter account. This also happens when you use outside applications to schedule your tweets.

It is a good idea to go in every now and then and revoke access to anything you no longer use.

Widgets:

This will be covered separately.

Doable 3 – Background Design

You will want to change the default background image. Ideally to a professionally designed one that matches your website and other social media platforms. This way you can brand it and make it unique to yourself. As you can see below, I have had mine professionally designed.

If you are not in a position to have one designed or you want to wait a while, there are some great resources for your background right inside Twitter. You can simply click on one of the pre-designed ones shown below.

If you don't like any of those or don't want your account to look like it is brand new, you can design your own with Themeleon.

Click on the Themeleon link and gain access to thousands of different background options.

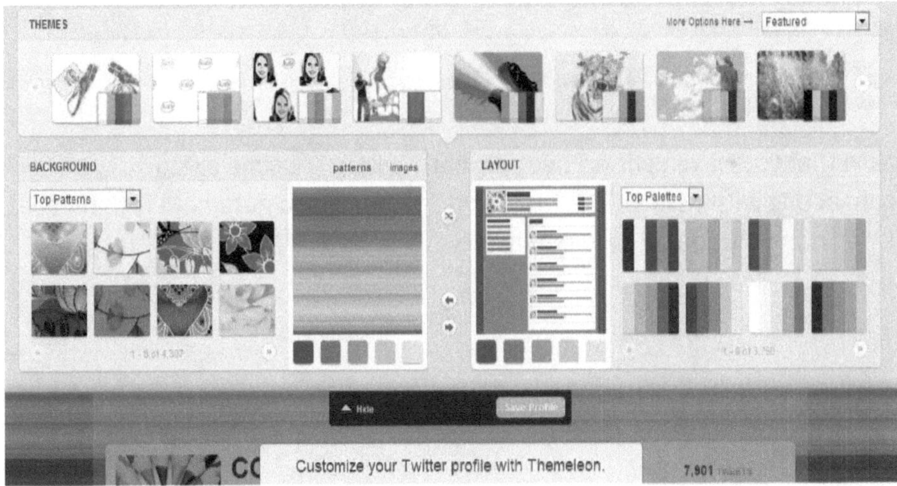

Simply scroll through all the options until you find one you like. Then click 'Save Profile' and it will update on your page.

I think the resources within Twitter are ideal if you are not getting a background designed yourself: the tools are flexible, user-friendly, creative and free. However, if you want to find alternatives, there are lots of sites that offer background creation services. You can simply search for 'Twitter Backgrounds' in one of the search engines.

Doable 4 – Start Connecting

Now that you have your account properly set up it is time to start connecting with people. The most important thing to note here is that each tweet can only contain 140 characters.

Not sure what to say? There is an example below - feel free to copy and paste it into Twitter. If you write your own tweet, make sure you tell me you are reading this book so I know how we became connected, and I can add you to the Twitter list I have made specifically for readers of this book. You can also use the hashtag #30dailydoables.

Doable 5 – Retweeting and Favorites

Retweets

When you see a tweet you think your followers would like, or be of value to them, you can retweet the post out to your followers. As you hover over a tweet some options will appear – Reply, Retweet, Favourite, Email Tweet.

Click Retweet and the tweet will open in a new box where you simply click the Retweet button.

It is always nice to thank people that have retweeted your content – you can do this either as a normal tweet with an @mention (this will be explained shortly), or in a Direct Message.

Be careful if you plan to retweet a post, from someone you don´t know, that has a link in it. Anything you retweet has your seal of approval, so if you retweet a bad link or something inappropriate, that will reflect on you. For people with whom I have built a relationship and trust their content, I retweet their links without checking them each time. It has taken quite a while to build up that trust, though. So, do keep that in mind when retweeting tweets with links.

Favorites

Making a tweet your favorite is similar to 'liking' something on Facebook. Everyone who follows you will be able to see the tweets you consider your favorites and the person who tweeted them will know as well.

I sometimes just favorite a tweet so I can read it, or what it is linking to, later.

To find all of your favourites click on 'Me' in the toolbar and then Favorites.

Doable 6 – What to Post

There are so many things you can tweet about. Remember, though, you only have 140 characters.

Here are just a few ideas:

- Images
- Quotes
- Jokes
- Tips
- Links to blog posts or your free offer
- Links to promotional materials
- Links to sales pages
- Contests
- Recommend someone

The possibilities are endless. The more you actively use Twitter the easier it will be to think of things to say. Consider Twitter like a text, except instead of texting one friend you're texting a group of friends. Remember to be yourself. Genuinely engage with others and it will make a big difference to your effectiveness on Twitter.

Things to think about when considering what to post:

What are your followers interested in?

What information do they want to know?

What are their questions?

What motivates them?

Give your followers a reason to continue following you!

This might be by posting links to information and products you think they will be interested in. It could be by posting anecdotal stories about what is happening with you and your business, or answering people's questions, or giving advice.

Make sure your Tweets aren't just a series of promotions. Yes, you can promote – but you also need to point people in the direction of free content, show off your knowledge and show off your passion. It is important to establish a marketing calendar so you can plan your tweets more strategically, in line with your goals.

Your followers are following you because they want to learn from you, always remember that.

Doable 7 – Posting

You may have reached out to me and rewteeted some people, but now you are going to post some tweets for yourself. Look through the list of ideas to post about and pick out a couple you are comfortable with – quotes are always a great choice if you are not sure what to do. Type or copy the tweet into the tweet section on your home page and click 'Tweet'. It is as easy as that! Wait a little while and then tweet out another one.

Doable 8 – @mentions, @replies and DMs

@Mention

A mention is any tweet that contains @username anywhere in the tweet.

Type a message and use @username instead of using a person's actual name. Once tweeted this turns into a link that people can click on, to go to that person's profile.

If you receive an @mention, that becomes part of a 'conversation'. You can read what has been previously posted by clicking on 'View conversation'.

People use @mentions to help promote other people.

Here are a couple of examples:

1. @friendsofsocial is promoting other users.

2. This person has just used my name to promote their own link (Please don't do that, it is really rude!).

3. @mariocoronatv is using a different way to retweet. He is retweeting my original post, but sending out 'via' me instead of with RT (retweet) at the front. It looks nicer if you retweet someone but take the time to change the tweet so it looks like the one above, instead of having RT at the front. Either one is fine, I just think the one with 'via @username' looks like a much neater tweet. I do use both types of retweets.

4. @troolsocial is promoting other users.

5.   @tournantinc has retweeted (see RT at the beginning) and is sharing one of my blog posts.

@Replies

If you would like to reply to a tweet, hover over the tweet and click the reply link. A new box will appear that starts with @username (the username of the person you are replying to).

To get the most exposure be sure to write something before the @username. If you start with the @username, only your mutual followers will see the tweet. If you have something written before the @username, then all of your followers and all of their followers will see the tweet.

Click on @Connect to see who has mentioned or replied to you. In this section you will see any time anyone has interacted with any of your tweets. It could be replying, retweeting, favoriting or just reaching out to you by using your @username.

When you come to Twitter this is the first place to visit, so you can thank people and reply to their messages.

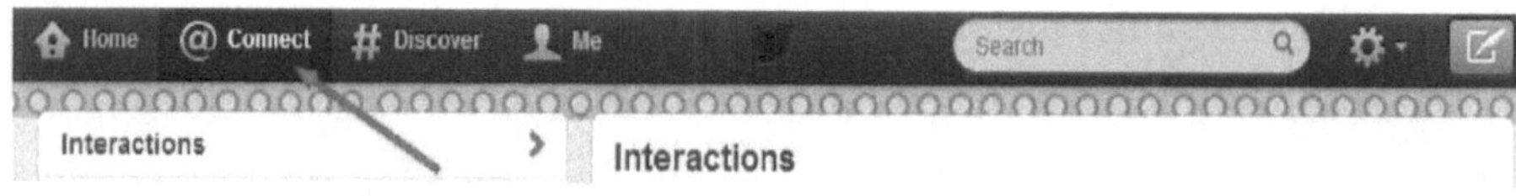

If you don't use their @username they will not know that you have sent them a tweet. Using mentions is a great way to connect with people and get noticed.

DM Direct Message

Direct Messages are private messages sent between two people – it is just like an email message. You can only send messages to people that are following you and only people you are following can send you a message.

To see who has messaged you or to reply to a DM, click on Settings and then Direct messages.

To send a DM to someone else go to their profile, click on the dropdown menu and click on Send a Direct Message.

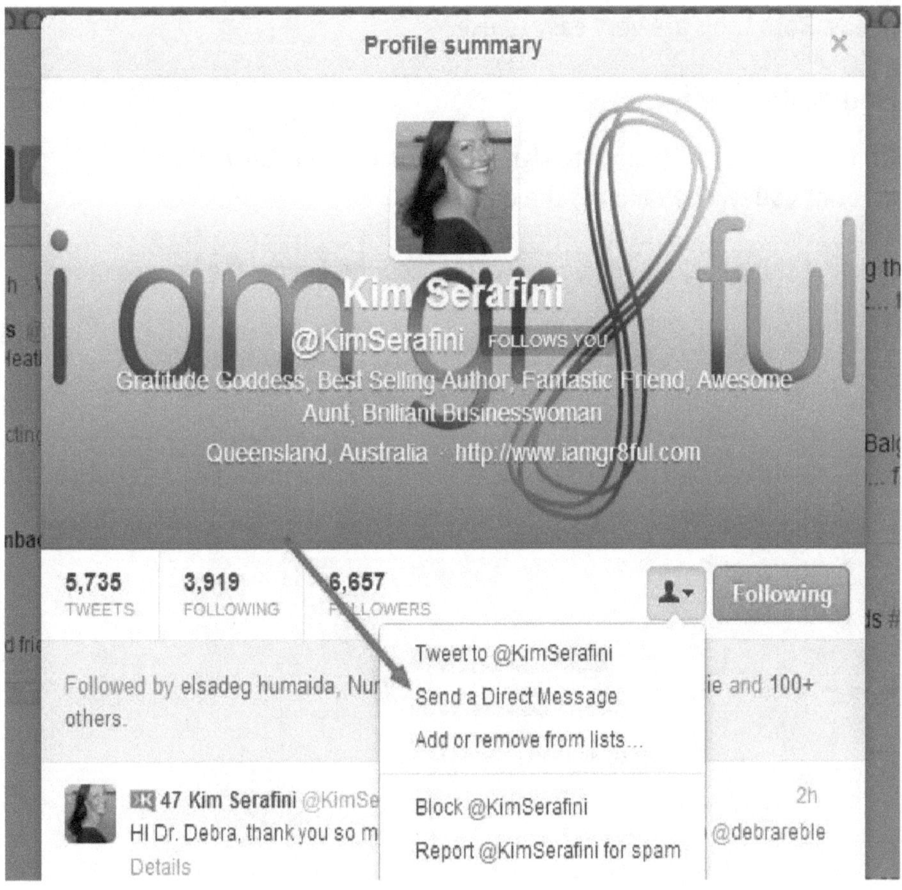

Doable 9 - Scheduling Tools

There are many tools you can use to schedule your tweets. I personally use Hootsuite and Buffer. Each of them has specific but mutually exclusive characteristics that are useful and that I like, so you may want to try both to see which service offers you the features most useful for your style and needs. Both tools are very easy to use.

Hootsuite

Go to www.hootsuite.com to sign up for an account. Once you have an account you will be taken to the dashboard.

The first thing to do is add your Twitter account. Follow the images here for details.

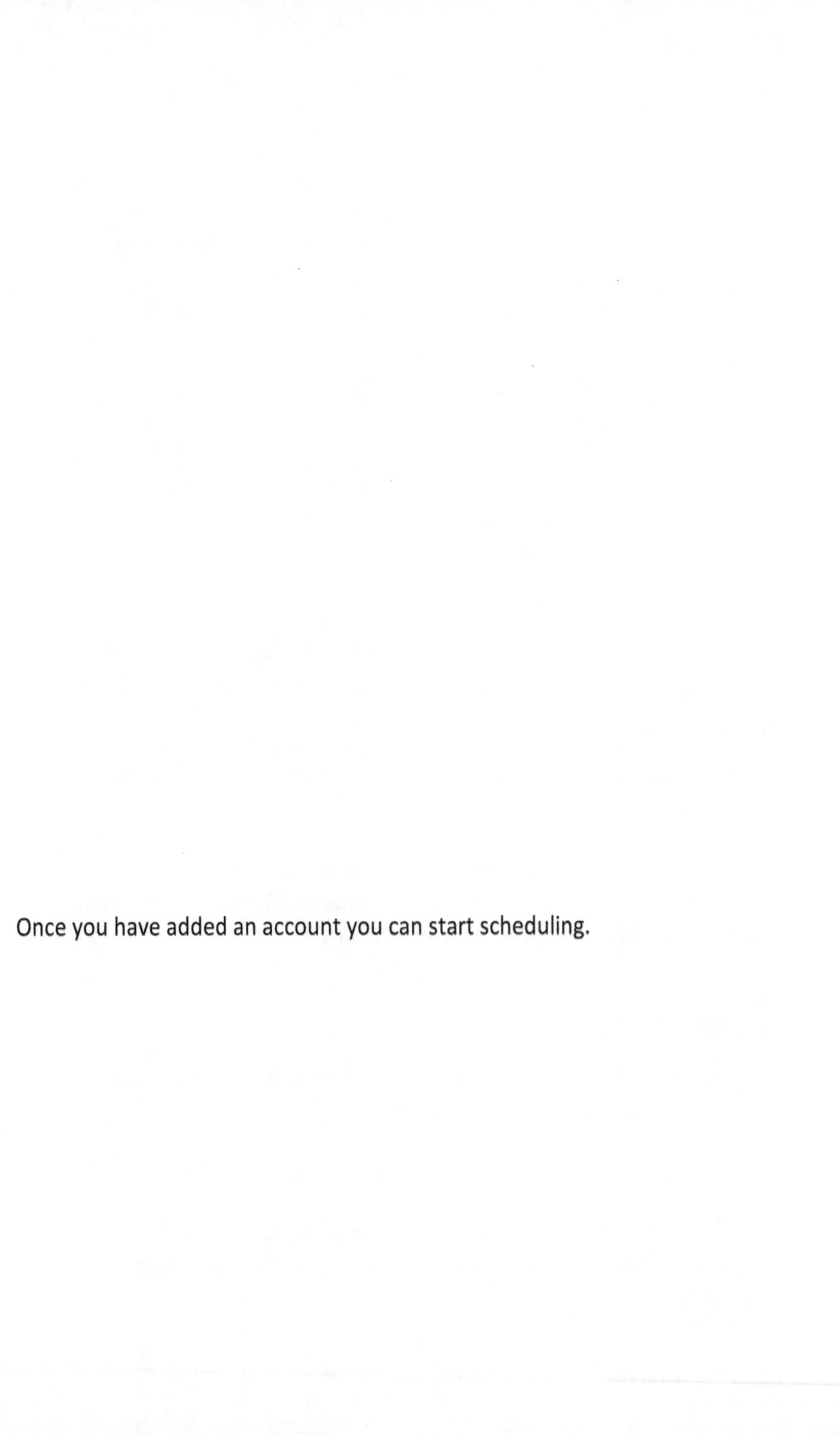

Once you have added an account you can start scheduling.

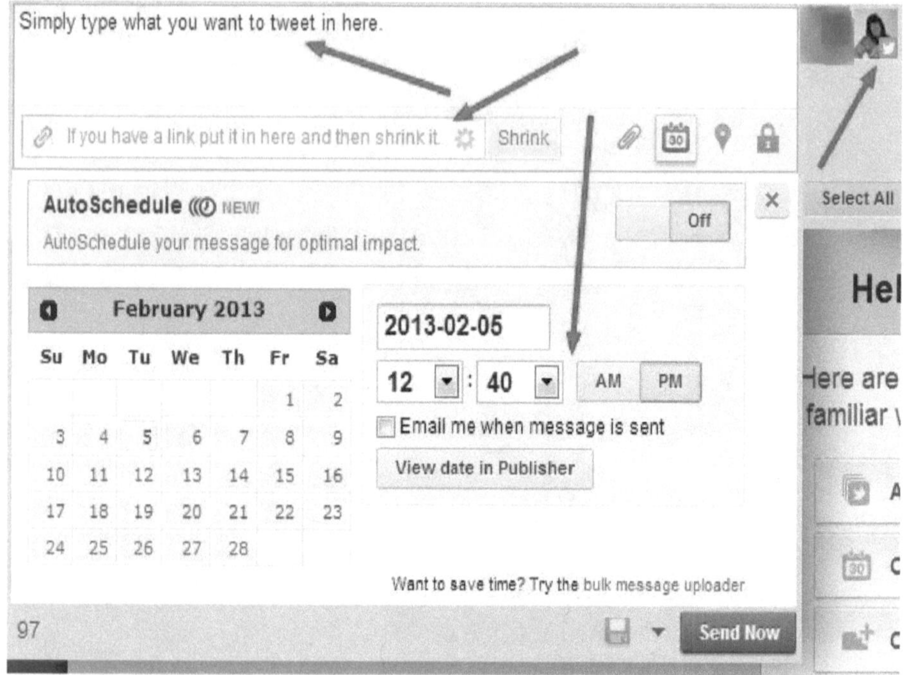

If you want to add an image simply click on the paper clip, choose your Twitter account, find the image on your computer and it will upload it to Hootsuite.

You can schedule a specific time for a tweet to go out or you can use autoschedule. With autoschedule, Hootsuite works out when will be the best time to tweet based on your previous tweets, and will send the tweets out then.

Buffer

Go to www.bufferapp.com to sign up for an account. Once you have an account you will be taken to the dashboard.

Add your Twitter account by clicking on the '+' next to Accounts.

Write your tweet in the update box and click on 'Buffer'. Your tweet will then go to the bottom of the list. Each time you add a new tweet it will go to the bottom of the list.

Move your tweets around by dragging them or clicking 'Shuffle'. Schedule the timings of the tweets in the 'Schedule' tab.

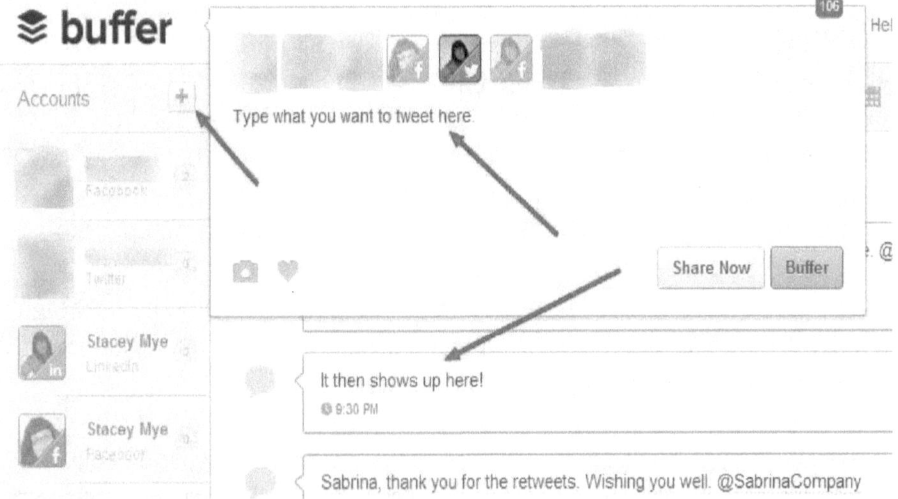

Doable 10 - Hashtags (#)

Hashtags(#) are used as keywords to make it easier to find people tweeting about a particular topic. Hashtags can be used for events, topics or other key pieces of information. I use the hashtag #30dailydoables for all of my training related to the Daily Doables.

If you search for #30dailydoables you will see all the tweets that people have sent using these hashtags. What is useful about searching with hashtags is that it will return tweets from all the people using the hashtag, *not just the people you follow,* so you can broaden your potential circle with people who have similar interests.

There is nothing you need to do to set up your own hashtag, you can just start using it. Search first to see if anyone else is using it. Just because they are doesn't mean you can't, but if you want something exclusive to you then you don't want other people to be using it.

Other hashtags, #TwitterTips for example, are ones that a lot of people use. So, if you did a search for that you would see the tweets from people all over the world using that hashtag.

If you see a hashtag and are not sure what it means, you can have a look at www.tagdef.com. Another useful place is www.hashtags.org; it is a massive collection of the hashtags that are in use.

Doable 11 – Lists

Twitter lists are a great way to prioritize your news feeds, keep track of the latest news and cut down the noise from your Twitter feed. You can group both the people that you follow, and those that you don't.

Key things to note about Twitter Lists:

- Can have up to 20 lists
- 500 people in each list
- Lists can be either public and private
- If you add someone to a public list they will be notified
- List names can be no longer than 25 characters
- List names cannot start with a number
- You do not have to be following someone to put them on a list
- Create your own lists or subscribe to other people's lists

Here are some ideas of Twitter lists you might like to create:

- People from an event you have been to or a course you are in
- Daily news in your industry
- Industry leaders
- Competitors (you might want to keep this one private!)
- Bloggers you follow
- Fans
- Friends
- Colleagues

To create a list; click on 'Me', Lists, Create list. This is also where you will manage your lists.

Add your List name, Description, and Privacy.

Create a new list   ×

List name	
Description	

Under 100 characters, optional

Privacy	⦿ Public · Anyone can follow this list
	◯ Private · Only you can access this list

Save list

Once you have saved your list, you can start adding people.

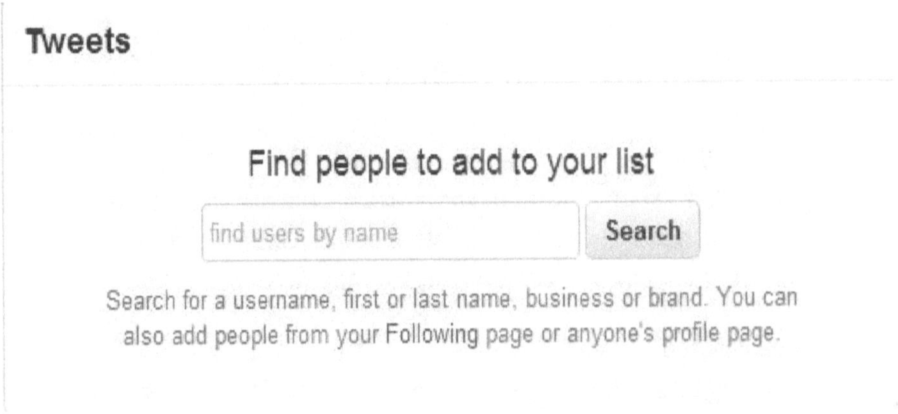

This is how you add people to a list from their Profile Page or Profile
Summary.

Doable 12 – Building Relationships Using Lists

In the previous Doable you learned about Lists. In this Doable you are going to add people to a list and let them know you have done that. It is great for building relationships. All you do is create a public list on a topic that is of interest to you and your readers. For this example we will use blogging.

Just say you created a list named 'Blogging Experts'. You add Anna Brown to the list and tweet her a message that says something like – 'I have added you to my Blogging Experts list, as you always share valuable tips on blogging. @theirusername ~shortlink to your list~'.

Be sure to add their name, so they receive the tweet and also a shortlink to your list. That way, other people that are interested in blogging may visit and subscribe to your list, and the person you added might like to share the list or go and see who else you think is a blogging expert.

Doable 13 – Link Shorteners

As you only have 140 characters you want to make the most of them. One way you can do that is to shorten the links that you share. When using a link, Twitter only allots you 120 characters instead of 140, regardless of the length of the link. If the link is too long Twitter will cut the end off. To avoid this use a link shortener.

You can see here what it looks like when your link is cut off.

This is how it looks if you use a link shortener.

There are various link shortener options available. The one I mostly use is www.bit.ly.

This tool shortens your website from: http://www.yourdomainname.com/the-name-of-the-blog-post to something like http://bit.ly/shortname.

The other thing useful about www.bit.ly is it gives you the ability to track how many people actually clicked on the link.

If you are using Hootsuite or one of the other scheduling tools, they have their own link shorteners.

Doable 14 – Twitter Search

You can search for all kinds of information on Twitter:

- People in your local area
- Others who share similar interests
- Who has tweeted about your business, brand or name
- People to follow

General Searching

You can search directly within your Twitter account. Search a specific word, hashtag or even someone's name by typing it in the search box and pressing 'Enter' or clicking on the magnifying glass.

Advanced Searching

For more advanced searching go to http://twitter.com/search.

Click on 'advanced search'

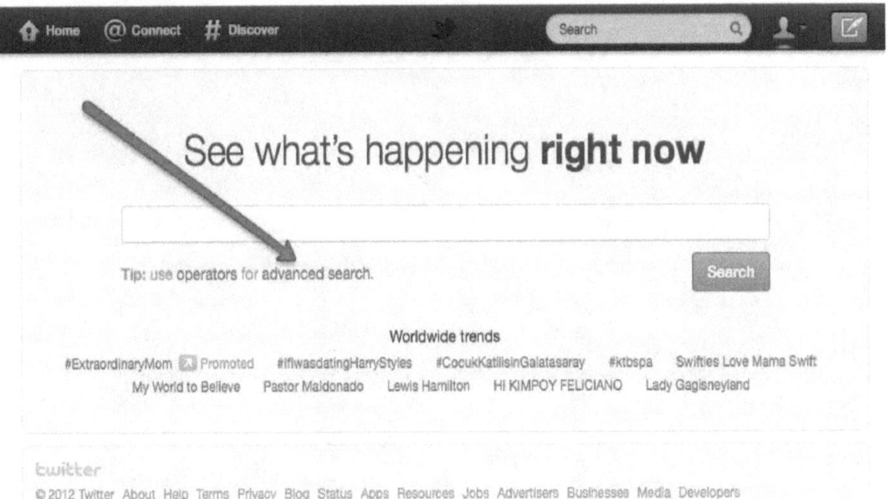

From here you have a number of ways to further narrow your search using words, people, places, and other variables. If you want to be even more specific in your search click on 'operators' and it will give you more ideas.

Advanced **Search**

Words

All of these words

This exact phrase

Any of these words

None of these words

These hashtags

Written in   Any Language

People

From these accounts

To these accounts

Mentioning these accounts

Places

Near this place

Other

Select   ☐ Positive :)   ☐ Negative :(☐ Question ?   ☐ Include retweets

[Search]

Doable 15 – Finding People to Follow

Now that you have everything set up, it's looking good and some posts are going out, it's time to invite people to your account/to follow you.

In the process of going through the Daily Doables you may have found people to follow on Twitter already. Maybe they've retweeted you, replied to you, started following you and in turn you have followed them as well. These are all passive ways of following people on Twitter.

You'll find as you use Twitter more frequently, you'll want to actively seek people to follow, and remove those who are not adding value to your Twitter feed.

Here are a few ways to find people to follow -

- Search for particular people that you already know about

- Click on the social media connect buttons on people's websites

- Twitter suggestions

- #Discover

- Find people in your industry whose followers would be interested in what you are doing, and start following them

- Follow people back

There are also quite a few Twitter directories (similar to the white or yellow pages). I have listed a few here but if you search for Twitter Directories in one of the search engines you will find a lot more of them.

- http://www.twellow.com

- http://justtweetit.com/

- http://www.tweetfind.com

Don't forget that the search feature in Twitter is also a great place to find people to follow.

One thing to keep in mind when following people is Twitter's follow limits. The first one is that you cannot follow more than 2000 people until more than 1800 people are following you. It is a good idea as you are building up your following that you keep your followers and following close in number. This will make it easier to get past the 2000 people limit.

Doable 16 – Starting Conversations

Starting conversations with strangers seems to be one of the scariest parts of being on Twitter. Once you start a few conversations you will feel much more confident with it. I find people on Twitter to be very friendly and usually will message back.

Retweeting and sharing someone's content is a great way to start a conversation. A lot of people will thank you for sharing and you can use that to continue the conversation.

Other than that you can just reach out to people – you can give them a 'shout out' (tell other people how great they are) if you have taken their course, or simply learned anything from them on Twitter or anywhere else.

Have a look at their bio and see if you have anything in common that you can use to start a conversation.

Just get out there and do it, it will become easier, I promise!

Doable 17 - Saying Thank You

'Please' and 'Thank You' go a long way in building relationships on Twitter - just like in the offline world.

Anytime someone shares your content (your blog post, for example) or retweets you, you will want to thank them for doing that.

If people are sharing your tweets and you never thank them, they are not going to continue doing that for long. It is also a great way to build relationships with people that already think what you are talking about is great.

I actually have a private list of all the people that regularly share my content. I want to keep them happy so they continue to do that. How do I keep them happy? By sharing their blog posts and retweeting them.

If you are asking people to retweet your tweets, it is always nice to say 'please'. Asking for retweets is not something I do, but I know that people do get good results with it. All you need to do is add, 'RT please' somewhere in the tweet. Some people will use 'plz', instead of please.

Doable 18 – Be Retweetable

Instead of having to ask for retweets, make your tweets retweet worthy, and you won't have to worry about that.

Make your tweets 120 characters or less. This will leave 20 characters for someone to RT with a comment and also include their Twitter ID.

Have you seen a RT that ended with …? This could be for several reasons:

- The tweet had too many characters, not leaving enough room for a RT that would include the full message.
- The comment added to the RT was too many characters cutting off the original tweet.
- The Twitter ID added too many characters causing the original tweet to get cut off.

You don't want this to happen to your tweets, so keep it a bit shorter.

Provide valuable content that encourages, teaches, inspires, or makes people laugh.

What is it about someone else's tweet that has you retweet it?

Keep that in mind when writing your tweets and others will want to retweet you and engage with you.

As you get used to reading your Twitter stream, you'll soon discover faces that become familiar to you because they are frequent tweeters. You may even find yourself remembering their Twitter IDs. When you get to know other Twitter users, you tend to read what they are tweeting about, share their tweets, and engage with them by responding to what they have to say.

You in turn want to be the familiar face to someone else by tweeting frequently, so they get used to seeing you in their Twitter stream.

Doable 19 – #FollowFriday

Every Friday you will see all over Twitter – #FF or #FollowFriday. Follow Friday is used for people to recommend other Twitter users that they think people should be following. To participate in this, all you do is put that person's username and #FF or #FollowFriday in the tweet somewhere. It is a great way to build relationships with the people you are recommending – as hopefully they will respond by saying thank you and you can start up a conversation.

A common mistake people make is to put loads of usernames in a tweet, and no other content, and tweet that out. It looks something like this –

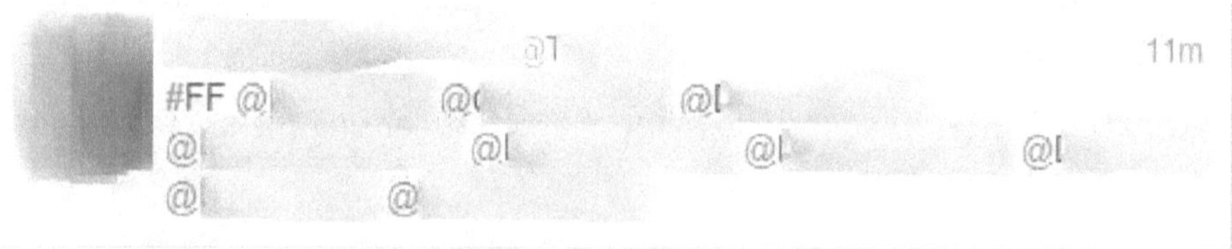

I do not think this is using the #FF concept to the greatest advantage. I never follow any of the people on the list when I see these kinds of posts. It is nice that someone would put you in such a post, but it does not yield many extra followers.

What works much better is if you say why you might want others to follow those people.

Examples:

Looking for other writers to network with – you should follow ...

Interested in social media – check out ....

Needing to work on your relationship...

At least then the names have some context and you can check them out if their area of expertise is of interest to you.

When you're included in a #FF tweet be sure to reply back, especially if they have given a reason for recommending you.

Doable 20 – Best Time to Post

There isn't a **best** time to post. It depends on your industry and where in the world the people you work with are.

I interact with people all over the world, so I have my tweets go out at various times through the day and night.

Some people say a good idea is to send them at 9am, 12pm, 3pm, 6pm and 9pm.

I personally think it is best to work out how many times you are tweeting each day and then spread those out over the times you want to be tweeting.

You can actually find out when people are responding the most to your tweets. But for right now just focus on making sure you are tweeting every day.

Doable 21 – Posting Images

To tweet an image directly from your Twitter account, click on the tweet box and then click on the camera image.

It will take you to your documents on your computer where you can select the image you'd like to tweet.

Be sure to add text otherwise all that will be in the actual tweet is a link. The image will drop down when people click on it.

Doable 22 – Trends

These are the most talked about news, topics or events at any given time. You can look at the trending topics in a particular location and also worldwide.

Twitter is being used more and more for breaking news. It's much faster to get the news out in a tweet than to write something up in the paper.

Watch the Trends and be the first to get the latest news, gossip, and reports.

You can find Trends directly from your home page.

You can also find trending topics at http://whatthetrend.com. This website shows up to the minute trending items along with all of the trends for the day.

If you have something relevant to add to one of the topics this is a great way to get exposure, as a lot of people are talking about the topic. Do not, however, just hijack a topic to get exposure. A couple of companies have done this to their detriment. Please only join in the conversation if you have something relevant to add.

Doable 23 – Website Widgets

Using a widget is a way to have your Twitter stream display on your website. You can see mine here:

People are able to follow you and interact with your tweets through this widget on your website.

To create your own widget, go to the Settings section in Twitter – click on Widgets and then Create New.

Choose a timeline source.

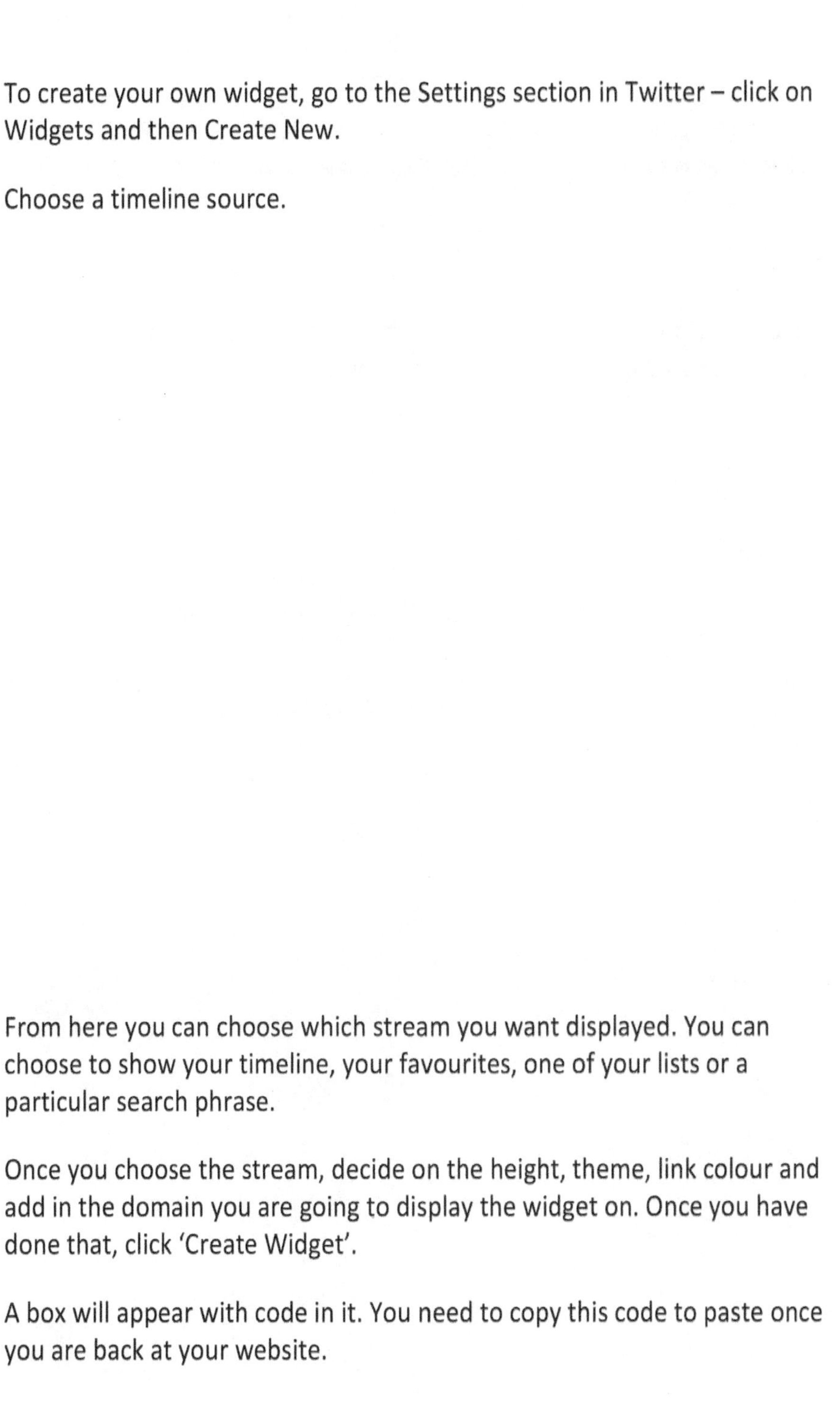

From here you can choose which stream you want displayed. You can choose to show your timeline, your favourites, one of your lists or a particular search phrase.

Once you choose the stream, decide on the height, theme, link colour and add in the domain you are going to display the widget on. Once you have done that, click 'Create Widget'.

A box will appear with code in it. You need to copy this code to paste once you are back at your website.

Copy and paste the code into the HTML of your site.

If you are on a self hosted WordPress website go to your Widget area, drag a Text box to the sidebar, copy in the code and click save.

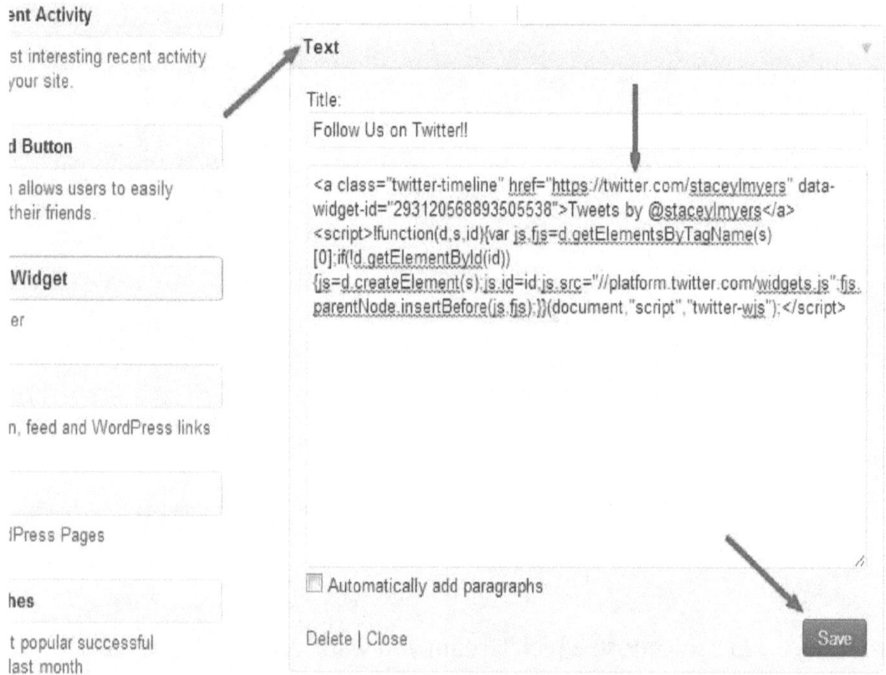

Doable 24 – Adding an Additional Link in Your Bio

As mentioned in Doable 2, when you set up your account you can add a link that you want people to go to. But a great way to help promote your free gift or course you are offering is to add an additional link in your actual bio. When adding this link you need to make sure that you use http:// and not just www. or it will not be a clickable link.

Doable 25 – Linking to Individual Tweets

Did you know each tweet has its own link?

This comes in handy if you wanted to reference a tweet in a blog post, article, social media update, book or eBook.

Here's how you can get the link to an individual tweet:

Click anywhere in the body of the tweet and it will open the tweet out.

Click on 'Details'

You'll then be taken to a page where you see that tweet only.

From your web browser, copy the address. So now, any time someone clicks on the link or puts it in the browser they will be taken to this exact tweet.

Doable 26 – Managing Who You Follow

I use a great tool called <u>Manage Flitter</u> to manage my account. There is a free version and a premium version. In the free version you can unfollow people based on a set criteria – they still have the default Twitter egghead image, for example. With the premium version you can also use it to follow people. You can find people with a general search or by following the followers of other people, or even who they follow. This is a very handy tool and one you should definitely check out.

In the image below, on the left side, are all the criteria you can use to unfollow people. I do not unfollow people just because they aren't following me back.

Keep in mind that Twitter doesn't like you to follow too many people using an application outside of Twitter (such as Manage Flitter). If you currently only have a small account follow less than 50 people a day and if you have a few thousand people following you I still wouldn't follow more than 100 people a day using this or any other system outside of Twitter. You can, however, follow many more than that if you manually follow them inside Twitter.

Doable 27 – Promoting Your Account

Be sure to let people know about your account. You can do this in a variety of ways.

- Have a link on your business card.

- Put links on your website.

- Post a message about your Twitter account on other social networking sites you belong to – for example Facebook, LinkedIn, Pinterest.

- Put a link in your signature on forums, email messages and other relevant places.

- If you have an email list, send an email to your subscribers telling them about your Twitter account.

The link you will use is www.twitter.com/yourusername.

Doable 28 – Mobile Applications

If you want to tweet on the move there are mobile applications available for your smartphone or mobile device. Twitter does have its own application available as well.

There are so many options, the best thing to do would be to search for Twitter phone applications in one of the search engines. The search will bring sites with blog posts that include various reviews. You may also search specifically for Twitter phone application reviews.

Doable 29 – Twitter Time Management

I have found the best way to manage time on Twitter is to make sure you know what you are going to post in advance and, even better, have it already scheduled. I know I waste a lot of time if I just sit there looking at the screen wondering what I am going to post. But, if I have it all taken care of in advance, I can spend my time on Twitter actually engaging in conversations and interacting with people.

Doable 30 – Congratulations!

You have made it to the last Doable! Congratulations!

Your last task is to send me a tweet and tell me how wonderful you now are at Twitter.

Now all you need to do is keep tweeting out consistently, starting conversations and sharing great content.

Well done and I wish you all the best!!

If you have found this book useful I would very much appreciate it if you left me a review on Amazon.